GOOD WEED
BAD WEED

GOOD WEED
BAD WEED

Who's Who, What To Do, and Why Some Deserve a Second Chance
(All You Need To Know About The Weeds In Your Yard)

Nancy Gift

Photography by Sheila Rodgers

St. Lynn's press

PITTSBURGH

GOOD WEED BAD WEED

Who's Who, What to Do, and Why Some Deserve a Second Chance

ISBN-13: 978-0-9819615-6-9

Library of Congress Control Number: 2010937019
CIP information available upon request

First Edition, 2011

St. Lynn's Press . POB 18680 . Pittsburgh, PA 15236
412.466.0790 . www.stlynnspress.com

Typesetting – Holly Rosborough, Network Printing Services
Cover Design – Jeff Nicoll
Weed photography – Sheila Rodgers
Editor – Catherine Dees

Photo Credits
All photos in the book are © Sheila Rodgers, except for the left photo on p. 50, which is the author's.

Disclaimer: The author and publisher expressly disclaim any responsibility for any adverse effects occurring as a result of the suggestions or information herein, including the handling or consuming of plants named in this book.

Printed in China through Global PSD

This title and all of St. Lynn's Press books may be purchased for educational, business, or sales promotional use. For information please write:
Special Markets Department . St. Lynn's Press . POB 18680 . Pittsburgh, PA 15236

10 9 8 7 6 5 4 3 2 1

TABLE OF CONTENTS

INTRODUCTION

Weed identification guides can be intimidating. Most of them are sober affairs, with either complex keys that require a ruler and magnifying glass for navigation, or with organization by plant family (think Latin) – which are all very helpful to a professional but useless if your beginning point is **"I have no idea what this plant is."** This guide is designed for someone at exactly that beginning point, looking at his or her lawn and wondering whether it is infested or blessed – and what to do next. If you don't have a lawn yet, just a weedy yard, this book is for you, as well. You might be questioning whether you should go the traditional route, with grass seed and a contract with a maintenance company. Or maybe you'd simply like to know how to make peace with the weeds you've got.

Weeds can pop up anywhere, but the greatest concern for most of us is with that manicured, labor-intensive green expanse that we call our lawn. When uninvited guests take up residence in it, we've been conditioned to assume that something's wrong and needs to be fixed. Not necessarily. As you will discover in these pages, there are a number of very worthy (and lovely) weeds out there that provide low-

Biennial Thistle   **Dandelion**

maintenance, all-season color and texture, despite the fact that they weren't the plants you seeded there in the first place.

Though lawn care companies and lawn care products will offer to kill your weeds and maintain a smooth, green carpet, none of them will admit a glaring truth: not all those weeds are bad, and none of their products are capable of selectively sparing the good weeds after the bad ones are dead and gone.

WHO ARE YOU CALLING A WEED?

A weed, by classic definition, is simply a plant out of place. But in our language and culture, the idea of a "good weed" is an oxymoron, since a weed is always a bad thing and thus can't possibly be good. However, the terms "good weed" and "bad weed" are actually common in other cultures. In Spanish-speaking countries, for instance, this book's title might translate as simply *Bueneza/Maleza*. Traditional farmers in Central America know that some of the weeds will provide mid-season dinner, and some will help contribute nutrients for next year's crop. It is a weakness of the English language that weeds are universally unwanted. Instead, I use the word "weed" more like the weed science term "volunteer" – meaning a plant that comes up without being planted or encouraged. The plants in this book are common urban and suburban volunteers. To me, the bad weeds in a lawn context are the ones that are unsightly or prone to outcompete natives in nearby wild spaces.

WHAT'S INSIDE...

Good Weed Bad Weed is designed to provide you with a quick and easy reference and identification tool – weeds at a glance. For each weed I give a description, its benefits or drawbacks, and the best methods of control.

The categories: I have grouped the weeds into two main categories, **Good Weeds** and **Bad Weeds**, and I introduce them chronologically by season. However, not every weed fits neatly into one of those categories. In some cases (hawkweed, for one), choosing the good or bad label was difficult, because a plant can be a bully to natives in one region but not in another. And there are a number of other plants that have admirable qualities despite some negatives. So I've included a third category I'm calling **Not-so-bad Weeds**.

The photographs: The beautiful photography of fellow weed enthusiast Sheila Rodgers takes you up-close for easy visual identification.

The Recipes: In the spirit of discovery and adventure, I've gathered a roster of tasty weed recipes, like Strawberry Japanese Knotweed Pie, Foxtail Tabouli and more – which you'll find in the back of the book. Purslane Salad, anyone?

GODSPEED WITH YOUR WEEDS

I fully expect that some readers will disagree with me about the good/bad designations. Everyone will have a unique judgment (my mother-in-law still pulls her dandelions, and I still help her do it when I visit – but I don't pull them in my own lawn). Further, my designation of good, bad or not-so-bad is only relevant in a lawn, semi-manicured yard or flowerbed, and is not meant to apply to farm fields or any other landscape. Those are different places, and would have their own set of good and bad weeds.

This book can't kill your bad weeds, but it can help you know what to do with your good ones, and how to safely minimize the bad ones. I wrote about many of these weeds in my first book, *A Weed by Any Other Name,* where I laid out my heretical weed scientist's perspective that a weed is in the eye of the beholder. Now, with this guide, I hope you, the weed-lover-in-training, will walk out into your yard or lawn, make a few new friends in the plant kingdom, and figure out how to best help your weedy friends outcompete and outnumber your weedy enemies.

Let me know how you're doing. I'd really like to hear from you. You can find me online at **goodweedbadweed.weebly.com**; also on Facebook and on my blog at **weedsandkids.blogspot.com**.

Healall

BAD WEEDS

✻

NOT-SO-BAD WEEDS

GARLIC MUSTARD
(Alliaria petiolata)

Garlic Mustard

DESCRIPTION & LIFE CYCLE

A wildly invasive perennial with rough-edged, rough-textured, almost triangular leaves alternating up a smooth stem, topped by a cluster of small, white 4-petalled flowers, or, later, a cluster of upward-pointing, long (1" – 2") seedpods which explosively scatter small black seeds when ripe. Though the plant appears to die after seed set, it merely goes dormant, and a new shoot will arise from the plant again next year, reliably. If in doubt about identifying this plant, crush a leaf between your fingers and sniff: the garlic odor is quite strong, with a significant base note of fresh broccoli.

It bears a few low-growing leaves in winter, and in early spring may look similar to some of the low-growing mints. However, as the dandelions are setting seed, garlic mustard will begin flowering – even the smallest of plants will set a few flowers, as it is sensitive to temperature and day length both.

BENEFITS

The sole benefit is that it's edible. May be substituted for or added to any recipe with greens and garlic or onion. Makes particularly good pesto (see also the recipe for **Garlic Mustard Colcannon** on p. 87). Seeds may be harvested to make bio fuel, though the utility of this is more symbolic than practical, given the hand labor involved in harvest.

1

GARLIC MUSTARD

Garlic Mustard (young)

PROBLEMS

Spreads wildly via seed and root survival and is virtually impossible to eliminate except by hand-pulling. Older plants typically get quite large and set seeds prolifically. Reproductively, it makes rabbits look like nuns. Deer will not eat it; in fact, no animal reliably eats it, due to its garlic-mustard taste. Few insects will even bother to visit.

CONTROL

Hand-pulling is most effective and easy between late fall and early spring, which is also when garlic mustard is both at its tastiest (I find the frosts cut the bitterness a bit) and also nutritionally useful, since so few other greens are available in winter. Fortunately, garlic mustard typically is not a lawn weed (it doesn't tolerate mowing), though it will invade mulched edges of flowerbeds.

Classrooms of children can be employed for removal of this plant. I find second graders to be particularly interested, because they're usually told that they can't pick flowers and can be eager to be useful if the chore also feels like something slightly rebellious. In helping lead second-grade nature walks, I let the children know early that they can eat a leaf (many will try this, though almost none ask for a second helping), and in spare moments I encourage them to see how big a pile of garlic mustard they can pick as they go.

CANADA THISTLE
(Circium arvense)

Canada Thistle

DESCRIPTION & LIFE CYCLE

A painfully prickly plant with smooth stems. Late summer flowers are ½" – 1" in diameter, purple, fluffy and non-showy. This perennial thistle shoots out of the ground as the maple leaves are still expanding, growing tall quickly. May be distinguished from **biennial thistle** by the absence of a rosette overwinter and by the absence of prickles on the top surface of leaves.

While most thistles are biennial – will die after setting seed – this thistle would seemingly live forever, coming fresh from the ground each spring. After flowering, seeds form with windborne white fluff, similar to but not as puffy as a dandelion. What appears to be multiple plants may well be a single plant with multiple shoots and a single underground root system.

BENEFITS

Almost none. Although butterflies like the flowers and birds like the seeds, the biennial thistles have larger, more attractive flowers and more substantive seeds for the birds.

PROBLEMS

This is a tall, garden nuisance, requiring persistent pulling. You don't want to let it touch your skin, let alone go barefoot amongst these plants.

3

CANADA THISTLE

Bee on Canada Thistle Flower

CONTROL

Repeated pulling. Pulled (flowerless) stalks may be left on the soil surface as mulch. White household vinegar may be used to burn the leaves and stalk (but will also kill underlying plants).

Recommended strategy: Pull every visible stalk in sight, by grasping firmly at the base of the plant with strong leather gloves every week (or every other week) for at least a couple of months. The key here is repetition. If you do it right and the soil is loose, you'll get up to almost a foot of root, though denser soils will not yield much root. The goal is to kill the root by starving it of energy (rather than removing it, since getting the whole root is nearly impossible). Each time you pull the top, the root has to expend energy to send up a new shoot.

If soil is too dense for pulling, try using a dandelion prong. In my early experiences with Canada thistle, I often used a hoe, a real time-waster with this plant because the stalks are tough and fibrous, and aiming precisely at the base of the plant can take several whacks. Tilling or digging may simply move and separate root sections, each of which may go on to become a new plant. Calm persistence, rather than one-strike violence, is key in the battle with this weed.

4

CRABGRASS
Large or Hairy (Digitaria sanguinalis)

Crabgrass

DESCRIPTION & LIFE CYCLE

Crabgrass is a light-green, wide-bladed summer annual, emerging around the end of the spring frosts and reaching its peak growth during the heat of summer.   Blades (tops and bottoms) and stems have long hairs. Flowering stalk emerges in summer's hottest days, with a handful or two of long (4" – 7") strands from the top, which have the annoying habit of getting stuck between my toes when I walk barefoot in it. Crabgrass plants themselves may grow wide at the base, but do not re-root along the stem. At first frost, crabgrass begins to die, turning a bit purplish or orange before it fades to brown, and becomes a bare patch just in time for winter.

BENEFITS

None, really, either for wildlife, pollinators, or lawn ecology.

PROBLEMS

The biggest problem is that crabgrass is perfectly adapted to insinuate itself into lawns, and is therefore quite difficult to control.

CONTROL

One of the most effective organic controls is to apply corn gluten (available under a variety of brand names) in early spring. This product acts as a pre-emergent control, meaning that it keeps crabgrass from germinating.   However, corn

5

CRABGRASS

gluten will also prevent emergence of any newly seeded lawn grasses. The irony is that crabgrass infests bare patches, and the ultimate solution for bare patches is to seed a desirable perennial grass or other lawn species to fill them.

My personal strategy for dealing with crabgrass is simply re-seeding. Each fall, when it begins to die back, I seed more clover or lawn seed through the crabgrass patches. Each spring, I spread some compost on bare patches and then re-seed some more clover and grass (even, sometimes, wildflower mix). This approach is very cheap – probably $2 a season – and completely non-toxic. However, I do still have crabgrass in my lawn each summer, over five years after moving in, and corn gluten would be more effective. What compost and re-seeding accomplishes, though, is that I don't have any winter bare patches where the crabgrass was, thanks to the fall seed scattering.

My other strategy is to install raised-bed vegetable gardens where the crabgrass grows (which at my house is in the middle of my lawn), because crabgrass needs just as much sun as most vegetables.

Crabgrass (closeups)

FOXTAIL
*Giant (Setaria faberi); Yellow (Setaria glauca);
Green (Setaria viridis)*

Foxtail

DESCRIPTION & LIFE CYCLE

Early in summer, these three annual grasses are not easily distinguished by a novice, and close examination of stem and blade bases is necessary. (Stems of all three are hairless, but blade tops may have hair or not, depending on which foxtail is being examined) However, foxtails in general are easily identified when flowering and in seed by the foxy-looking flower: long, furry-looking (2" – 3" for green or yellow; 4" – 6" for giant), bristly spikes on stalks.

BENEFITS

Giant foxtail is the largest and softest of the flowers, but the smaller ones are still satisfying to pet, as long as you stroke them the right direction. Seeds are edible, like other small grains, and are cultivated in some parts of the world. May be substituted in amaranth or quinoa recipes, since these are also wild grains with small seeds. (See recipe for **Weedy Foxtail Tabouli** on p. 88.)

PROBLEMS

I think of foxtail as a bad weed, because when it takes over a field or garden it leaves very little room for other plants.

CONTROL

Newspaper and mulch can prevent emergence of foxtails; mowing can make its appearance

FOXTAIL

neater. Hoeing and other kinds of soil cultivation can kill foxtail easily in spring or early summer when the plant is still small, but by late summer the task is much harder, as the stems and roots can be quite tough. If you have any grass coming up in a vegetable or garden bed, early control is easier than waiting until after it goes to seed – and foxtail, in particular, seeds prolifically.

MORE ABOUT...

It bears the single most appealing and recognizable grass seed head for children to play with, both the giant and the smaller forms. Edibility aside, I wouldn't encourage anyone to cultivate foxtail, because I'm fairly certain we can find all we want to eat of it just by gathering it from roadsides and weedy cultivated areas.

Foxtail Flower

POISON IVY
(Toxicodendron radicans)

Poison Ivy

DESCRIPTION & LIFE CYCLE

Poison ivy is a perennial, spreading vine whose leaves, branches and roots produce an oil that can cause a painful, itchy rash – for some, after even the slightest exposure. Growing on a tree, poison ivy's dominant feature may be a thick, hairy stem, bound tightly to the tree trunk; the hairy stem is a great identifying tool, as no other common woodland vine resembles it. Leaves are in threes, with a symmetrical, long-oval middle leaf, and outer leaves often somewhat mitten-shaped, with more lumps on the outside of the leaf than toward the center. However, poison ivy leaves are highly variable in shape, some almost perfectly smooth-edged, some with lots of rounded "teeth" or indentations. In early spring, leaves are glossy and reddish or purplish, making them camouflage with soil. Seedling poison ivy has fairly large (½" – 1" long and wide, spade-shaped) cotyledons. Easily confused with box elder, a cousin of sugar maple, which also has leaves in threes, but which grows up straight, lacks a hairy stem, and emerges as a bright, light green in early spring. Also commonly confused with Virginia creeper because of the glossy reddish color in early spring, but Virginia creeper has five leaflets, and non-hairy vines.

BENEFITS

A native plant in the U.S., poison ivy's berries are an excellent winter food source for birds – small comfort to anyone who has suffered the painful consequences of touching one of these plants.

POISON IVY

Poison Ivy with Jewelweed

PROBLEMS

The biggest is the painful, itchy effect of its oils on our skin when we come in contact with the leaves, branches or roots. Many people have inhaled the oil's vapors (especially when burning the plant for disposal) and experienced a severe reaction. Many of the "bad" qualities of poison ivy are shared by poison oak and poison sumac. An authoritative web site for all three is *www.poisonivy.us*.

CONTROL

Best controlled in early spring when it is young, before other foliage hides it and its glossy, reddish leaves have such a distinctive appearance. In its first couple of years it may be easily controlled by pulling – with gloves and long sleeves, of course. Pants, socks, and closed-toe shoes are recommended before tackling it in a wooded area. Trailing, ground-level vines may be pulled gently and firmly to remove not only the visible shoot but the twine-like root, which lies typically at or slightly under less than an inch underground or at the soil surface.   Older plants require vigilant, multi-season action, beginning with sawing through the trunk of the ivy stem as close to the ground as possible, followed by regular examination of the trunk base, where repeated sprouting from the root is likely. Don't even think of using a Weedeater, since it will just scatter bits of the plant everywhere. All products advertised for its control, including full-strength vinegar, will be toxic to surrounding plants as well.

COMMON RAGWEED
(Ambrosia artemisiifolia)

Ragweed (young)

DESCRIPTION & LIFE CYCLE

Ragweed is a summer annual, emerging soon after the last frost, growing slowly for early summer, and sending out its evil, nasty pollen from nondescript, spike-shaped green flowers in midsummer. Leaves are lacey and divided, and are shaped a great deal like marigold leaves, except their color tends to be lighter green than marigold's, almost gray. Though ragweed will grow 2 to 3 feet tall in open areas without competition, it may grow up to 4 to 5 feet tall when trying to outcompete taller plants such as corn.

BENEFITS

Ragweed may have some medicinal uses, but its tendency to provoke allergies doesn't make it worth keeping around for the medicine cabinet. It is not edible, not good for any beneficial insects or wildlife, and it is not attractive.

PROBLEMS

Mowing will make ragweed shorter and less vigorous, but will not kill it or keep it from flowering.

CONTROL

Pulling and hoeing are highly effective, but both are more pleasant activities when the plant is young, especially before flowering. However, even pulling it at flowering is better than letting it go to seed. Mulching will reduce ragweed seed emergence in spring.

11

COMMON RAGWEED

MORE ABOUT...

Be aware that strong allergies to ragweed may extend into allergies to related herbs, such as chamomile. Ragweed may be confused with mugwort *(Artemisia vulgaris)*, which tends to grow taller, and has less-divided leaves. Mugwort leaves have a more pleasant odor, and mugwort generally has more medicinal uses. Giant ragweed *(Ambrosia trifida)* has a three-lobed leaf, somewhat like a webbed bird's footprint, and can easily grow 7 to 8 feet tall.

Ragweed

Mugwort (look-alike)

JAPANESE KNOTWEED
(Polygonum cuspidatum)

Japanese Knotweed

DESCRIPTION & LIFE CYCLE

A very large, invasive weed, never in lawns but very likely on the edges of lawns and in shrubbery. Its spade-shaped leaves alternate along a tall (4 to 8 feet) jointed stem; bare stems in winter look like slightly zig-zagged bamboo. Flowers are small and non-descript, but appear in a spray of white along the ends of stems in late summer.

BENEFITS

Introduced as an ornamental for its striking shape and white influorescence. Honeybees love this plant and make a dark, thick honey from its blooms. Edible in its early stages (look for its shoots when daffodils are blooming), and may be prepared like rhubarb or asparagus (see recipe for **Strawberry Japanese Knotweed Pie** on p. 90).

PROBLEMS

Tenacious, fast-spreading and invasive, it is extremely difficult to get rid of or even manage. Spreads quickly (by seed and by underground) into wild areas.

CONTROL

No individual herbicide will kill it, even if I were recommending herbicide. Some unnamed gardeners I know sunk a pot of it in their garden,

JAPANESE KNOTWEED

Japanese Knotweed

thinking it was a possible new ornamental. When I saw the knotweed two seasons later, we tried to remove it, which turned out to be more of a battle than just pulling out the pot. After we yanked the plant we dug a hole almost 3 feet deep and equally wide around and under the where the pot had been, filled the hole with fresh soil (free of stray knotweed roots, we hoped), and now, over a year later, the plant still tries to come back.

What I'm saying is, digging alone doesn't work. A possible solution: First, cut existing stalks to ground level (or dig them out). Cover soil with a layer of black plastic, topped with carpet, topped with more black plastic, another layer of carpet, and a final layer of black plastic. Now, let sit for five years, all while watching for the knotweed to spread from the edges of the barrier. Note that this plant is rumored to spread over 10 feet under concrete roads and sidewalks, though I can't confirm this fact. Fortunately, it will not creep into mowed areas, but once it is present, few mowers can even be driven into a stand of it, because it is so tall and tough-stalked.

In other words, DO NOT INTRODUCE THIS PLANT. And if you see it coming your way, be ready for a serious long-term battle with it, unless you want it to overtake your life.

POISON HEMLOCK
(Conium maculatum)

Poison Hemlock

DESCRIPTION & LIFE CYCLE

This highly toxic plant is easily confused with **Queen Anne's lace**. Poison hemlock is a biennial, with feathery leaves forming a ground-level rosette in its first year, and shooting into an adult-height stalk the second. Its leaves are less feathery and more fern-like than Queen Anne's lace, however. Leaf bases and stalks are hairless, often with purple streaks or spots. Stalks, unlike Queen Anne's lace, are substantial – about as thick as a thumb; flowers bloom earlier, beginning in June or even very late May. Flower heads are white and umbrella shaped. In a lawn, this plant does not get established easily, but can grow in gardens and in overgrown lawn edges.

BENEFITS

Flowers are an excellent source of food for many pollinators (including the Black Swallowtail butterfly) and beneficial wasps.

PROBLEMS

This plant is highly toxic to eat, even in small quantities. This, not the hemlock tree, is the plant that Socrates consumed in his state-ordered suicide. It is particularly a scourge in pasture, rendering the areas around it unfit for grazing.

15

POISON HEMLOCK

Poison Hemlock

CONTROL

Regular lawn mowing will typically control this plant, but if the area is not to be mowed, then repeated pulling may be needed. Mulch will not help. Poison hemlock likes wet soils, but will also grow in clay soils and drier areas, such as in new construction.

MORE ABOUT . . .

Poison hemlock can also be confused with water hemlock (which has more purple, sheathed leaf bases, and is also highly toxic), **yarrow** (which is a smaller plant, with more feathery, delicate leaves), and wild parsnip (which has thicker leaves and yellow flower heads).

FLEABANE
(Erigeron philadelphicus)

Fleabane

DESCRIPTION & LIFE CYCLE

The biennial or perennial fleabane is the least attractive member of the daisy clan. Fleabane leaves are 4" – 6" long, hairy, and the flower shoot can easily exceed a foot in height, but with only tiny (½") flowers. Fleabane petals are slender, almost threadlike. Flowers in late spring and throughout early to mid-summer.

BENEFITS

Fleabane's visual appeal is limited, at least compared to other daisies, and it grows tall so quickly, it may make lawns with it look ragged.

CONTROL

Fleabane thrives in poor, rocky soils, and is not terribly competitive in healthy, dense turf. Both mowing and pulling should manage it sufficiently.

Alternatively, you can help reduce its presence by enriching the soil with compost and seeding clover or grass. Fleabane is not terribly competitive with dense stands of either lawn turf or meadow species; it thrives best in areas that have little else growing.

MORE ABOUT...

I consider fleabane less desirable than many other lawn flowers in part because its bloom is such a disappointment compared with other daisies. My daughters have included fleabane blooms in many

17

FLEABANE

bouquets, but, like **dandelion**, its bloom is quick to fade, and by the time I've put it in a hastily poured vase of water, it is already drooping, its petals beginning to brown. I give fleabane credit that it doesn't spread wildly, however, and so it really doesn't generally merit a vigorous eradication campaign. Instead, I find the plant so forgettable that when I see those fuzzy, oval leaves in spring, I always spend at least a couple of days hoping it is going to turn out to be something lovely. Then, a bud forms, thready petals curled up on top, and I remember: it is only fleabane.

Fleabane Buds and Flowers

HAWKWEED
(Heiracium aurantiacum)

Hawkweed

DESCRIPTION & LIFE CYCLE

Hawkweed is a perennial flower with a hairy rosette of oval-to-strap-like leaves. Flowers, which bloom in early summer, are brilliant orange, roughly 1" across, often with reddish centers and lighter orange outer petals. Stalks bear few leaves but several flowers, usually only one to two blooming per day.

BENEFITS

The brilliant color of the flowers makes their scraggly appearance in a lawn worth the trouble of mowing around them. Bees and other small pollinators also enjoy its blooms.

CONTROL

In western mountains and some parts of East coast, hawkweeds are invasive, and researchers are working on biological control options to prevent its spread in wild regions. Mowing flower heads will reduce their scraggly appearance, and it typically only sends one flower stalk per year. As with many lawn perennials, control could include pulling (though the entire root must be removed for full control) – or newspaper and mulch or topsoil to smother a patch of it, if you really wanted rid of it. Because of its potential to be invasive, I do not recommend introducing this plant as an ornamental to your garden.

This is an example of one of the many plants introduced from Europe for its beauty, but which seem to thrive beyond where it is wanted here

HAWKWEED

Hawkweed

in North America. It is unpalatable to grazing animals and is therefore not desirable in pasture. However, it is also unrealistic to think this plant can be eradicated. I view this plant with affection and tolerance in suburban ecosystems; spraying it would be just as undesirable as spreading it, in my opinion. Hawkweeds that volunteer in lawns are simply beautiful, so we might as well enjoy them.

Hawkweed Stem (closeup)

PROSTRATE KNOTWEED
(Polygonum aviculare)

Prostrate Knotweed

DESCRIPTION & LIFE CYCLE

Prostrate knotweed, as its name implies, is another extremely low-growing plant, a summer annual, which emerges just after tree leaves are on. Prostrate knotweed, like other Polygonum **(lady's thumb,** Pennsylvania smartweed, **Japanese knotweed,** curly and broadleaf dock), has an ocrea, or thin membrane, surrounding the base of each leaf, though this is hard to see on this very small plant. Leaves are alternate along green stems, each looking a bit like very short grass blades. Flowers are nondescript, about the size and shape of a drop of spring drizzle, and may be pink or white. Prostrate knotweed can be distinguished from **prostrate spurge** by the paired, opposite leaves on spurge.

BENEFITS

Prostrate knotweed will grow on farm roads and other highly compacted soils.

CONTROL

Since this plant likes compacted soil so well, one would be hard-put to find a replacement plant. Usually, this plant doesn't require control, but it does form a taproot, so control would generally need to including finding and removing at least a portion of root. (This can be tricky since a single

PROSTRATE KNOTWEED

Prostrate Knotweed Foliage

plant can spread so widely.) The best solution, if it is unwanted in a lawn, is competition from vigorous perennial lawn species, under which prostrate knotweed will not germinate well. In a lawn, any solution would also have to include dealing with the underlying soil compaction problem, which this plant indicates.

MORE ABOUT...

I've seen prostrate knotweed in almost every occasional-use farm road I've ever walked on. This plant nearly earns "good weed" status for preventing washout erosion on such roads. However, it is not edible, medicinal or particularly beautiful, and I would say that its presence in a lawn is less desirable than almost any perennial plant.

PROSTRATE SPURGE
(Euphorbia maculata)

Prostrate Spurge (young)

DESCRIPTION AND LIFE CYCLE

Extremely low-growing summer annual, with small (¼" to ½" long) leaves opposite one another along curving, spreading stems. Leaves of the spotted spurge *(Euphorbia prostata)* have a purplish splotch in the center. Stems are fibrous, and flowers, such as they are, are extremely nondescript: tiny white flowers, very close to the leaf bases. When a leaf is pulled or a stem broken, white milky sap will seep out.

BENEFITS

Its benefits are definitely mixed. In the Southwest, spotted spurge is reputed to be a topical treatment for rattlesnake bite. **However, this plant is poisonous if ingested by mouth.**

CONTROL

These plants thrive in dry places, the cracks between bricks or in sidewalks, and on mulched surfaces. Though this plant isn't exactly doing any harm in most of these places, as a rather weak annual, it isn't even doing much to prevent erosion. Pulling works, of course, and newspaper topped with mulch would also kill it in a garden area, if it is even worth worrying about at all.

23

PROSTRATE SPURGE

MORE ABOUT...

I thought about putting this one with the "good weeds" because of its audacious ability to grow where no plant has grown before. However, audacity alone isn't exactly a benefit, so I have relegated this fairly harmless weed to this section, just because it has so little to say for itself. It is a cousin of poinsettia. Easily confused with **prostrate knotweed**, which has alternating leaves that are more pointed at their tips.

Prostrate Spurge

BIENNIAL THISTLE
Bull Thistle (Circium vulgare)
Musk Thistle (Carduus nutans)

Biennial Thistle (mature)

DESCRIPTION & LIFE CYCLE

Painfully prickly plants, with low-growing leaves in a rosette in their first year; in their second year capable of rising to over 3 feet tall, with glorious fuzzy-looking pink or purple blooms. Leaves have rough edges (dandelion-like in outline) and are prickly all over – tops, bottoms, edges of leaves.

In their birth year, or in a lawn where regular mowing prevents growth of a vertical stalk, this plant is simply an annoyance for those who walk barefoot on their lawns. Stepping on a plant (or attempting to pull it bare-handed) is an excruciating experience not easily forgotten. In their second year (or when released from the pressure of weekly mowing), biennial thistles will grow tall, forming multiple branches and large blooms. After seed formation, plant will die, and no new rosette of leaves will form (though seeds are prolific).

BENEFITS

Many of these biennial thistles are native plants, edible by goats (unfortunately in short supply in most suburbs), and their large flowers are extremely attractive to butterflies. Seeds are a nutritious, tasty food for many birds, including charming dandelion-yellow goldfinches. Slow-growing and low-growing in the lawn, a single plant can survive for years without reproducing, but if allowed to flower and seed, will be visually attractive without requiring you to do anything but watch.

BIENNIAL THISTLE

Bee on Biennial Thistle Flower

CONTROL

A dandelion prong is highly effective. Simply dig enough to separate the leaves from the roots, and use the prong to put the prickly rosette in the compost. Mulching is not effective. Winter is an excellent time to remove thistle plants, especially if you're already wearing thick gloves.

MORE ABOUT...

In our first year in this house, I had a "watch and see" approach to all garden plants, unless I knew them to be weeds. Since then, we've had one or two thistles in our lawn per year, and I'm always tempted to let one grow, but I think I'll probably wait until one volunteers in the flowerbed, instead.

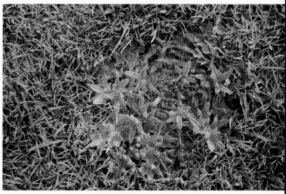

Bull Thistle (young)

NUTSEDGE
Yellow (Cyperus esculentus)
Purple (Cyperus rotundus)

Nutsedge

DESCRIPTION & LIFE CYCLE

As the saying about grasses goes, "Rushes are round; sedges have edges." This sedge, like others, has a triangular base (relatively easy to feel, harder to see without cutting off the leaves), so that blades emerge from three sides (most lawn grasses produce blades either on two sides of their shoot, or all around the shoot). Nutsedge is lighter green than lawn grasses, and tends to grow in wet areas, though it may grow in a variety of soils. Flower is a round, tan (yellow nutsedge) or reddish/purplish (purple nutsedge) cluster or clusters of anthers (about the size of fingernails clippings, but straight), and appears in late summer. (The two species are very difficult to distinguish, but they grow so similarly that telling them apart isn't really necessary.) Nutsedge reproduces primarily via tubers, which form in late summer as nodes on the roots. The tubers are perennial.

BENEFITS

The tubers (nutlets) are edible, with a nutty taste, and may be eaten raw or cooked.

CONTROL

Pulling or smothering with newspaper and mulch works best. In a lawn, this is probably not worth controlling, but in a garden, tubers will spread – this plant gets harder to eradicate the longer it has been allowed to thrive, due to the spreading nutlets. Do NOT plow or till this weed under,

27

NUTSEDGE

because that simply spreads the tubers, and plowing a patch of it is likely to move tubers throughout the garden.

MORE ABOUT...

I have a patch of nutsedge at the bottom of our lawn that I have allowed to thrive for years. I also have a reliable but small number of nutsedge plants that emerge each year in my vegetable garden, despite years of consistent pulling; however, as long as I keep pulling they don't take over the garden. I believe that nutlets are left behind when I pull the plants. I'm careful to pull nutsedge especially thoroughly before I dig for potatoes, so I don't spread it while digging. I've never had a large enough patch of nutsedge to make the tubers worth harvesting and eating, though I'd like to try them someday.

Nutsedge (closeup)

Nutsedge Seedhead

28

BINDWEED
Field (Convolvulus arvensis)
Hedge (Calystegia sepium)

Bindweed

DESCRIPTION & LIFE CYCLE

Both of these weeds are perennial vines with round white blossoms, often mistaken for their close cousins, the **morning glories**. Bindweed leaves are arrow-shaped, with longish, parallel sides and a pointed tip. On field bindweed, which has smaller flowers and leaves, leaf tips are a bit rounded, and the leaf base is curved; hedge bindweed leaves are more sharply angled, especially at the base. Field bindweed flowers are the size of a quarter or half-dollar, while hedge bindweed flowers are large, opening to about the size of a standard coffee cup mouth.

BENEFITS

May be considered attractive, by bees as well as humans.

CONTROL

These plants are hard to control, in part because their roots twine underground much as the shoots twine above. Repeatedly cutting the plant off at the base will eventually kill it, but persistence is required, especially if the plant is large and thriving when you first attempt to eliminate it. Field bindweed can be harder to eliminate because it may be hard to find where the vine enters the ground, and a large infestation probably includes several plants.

29

BINDWEED

Bindweed (young)

MORE ABOUT...

Bindweed, both types, can be serious problems in crops or pastures, as neither is edible by grazers, and they can both make harvest (cutting hay or combining grain) difficult by tangling up in the equipment. Though perennial, neither maintains their green color all year, so they can interfere with the growth of a lawn but leave the ground bare in winter. Also, they can damage hedges by slow strangulation. However, their attractive flowers may make them worth the downsides in some particular locations. Trellising may be a reasonable way to guide their growth away from nearby plants and still leave the flowers for you to enjoy.

MORNING GLORY
Ivyleaf (Ipomoea hederacea)
Tall (Ipomoea purpurea)

Morning Glory

DESCRIPTION & LIFE CYCLE

These are summer annual vines, emerging as large, nearly heart-shaped cotyledons in early summer, and twining higher throughout summer until blooming around the time school starts in fall. Morning glory dies back with first frost. Its leaves – either three-lobed (ivy leaf) or spade-shaped (tall) – alternate along the stem, the flowers emerging singly from just above the base of each leaf. Flowers are large and round, shaped like a shallow trumpet, ranging from pink to blue to violet, though some red morning glory species are present in the South. Confused most commonly with **bindweed**, which is usually seen without cotyledons, since it is perennial. Blooms best in east light, as the name implies.

BENEFITS

Morning glories are cultivated by many gardeners for their showy flowers.

CONTROL

The annual morning glories can most easily be controlled by breaking them off at the base (hoeing or pulling), near the soil surface. Extracting the root is not necessary, since these are annual, and don't have enough root reserve to re-grow after the shoot is pulled. Mulching, unless very thick

MORNING GLORY

Morning Glory (young)

or impermeable (like newspaper or black plastic), does not control them, as their large seeds enable them to come up through thin layers of mulch.

MORE ABOUT...

Morning glory, like bindweed, is a real scourge for mechanical harvesters on large-scale farms, tangling plants together and then tangling up the machinery. However, seeds fall within easy range of the adult plant, and are too heavy to travel by air, too smooth to be carried by animals. Therefore, if morning glory is gracing your garden, it isn't going to cause trouble for anyone else. Morning glory can be your own private pleasure, no matter now many lists of bad agricultural weeds it makes. Its cotyledons are easy to recognize, and if the morning glories are ever undesirable later, hand-pulling or hoeing them – at least on a garden scale – is easily done.

Morning Glory (mature)

GOOD WEEDS

WILD GARLIC/WILD ONION
(Allium ursinum / Allium crispum)

Wild Garlic Bulbs

DESCRIPTION

A grass-like, perennial plant with each leaf round and tube-like. The odor is strongly like onion/garlic when picked. Most visible from fall to early spring, but may be seen year-round. The root consists of a small white bulb, very similar to scallions in the grocery store. Wild garlic has a bit of papery membrane around the base of the stem, which might then branch into different leaves; wild onion leaves are more typically green right down to the soil surface.

LIFE CYCLE

This plant spreads primarily by roots. Tilling can spread it, but new bulbs can sprout and multiply from existing bulbs, much the way daffodil clumps will grow and spread. Flowers are not often seen in lawns and gardens, but would appear as a cluster of white, lily-like 6-petal flowers.

BENEFITS

Edible – an excellent substitute for chives, scallions, garlic, or small amounts of onion.

CONTROL

Pulling the whole plant, including the root, removes it, but is difficult to do in dense soil. Pulling tops repeatedly slows it down, and may prevent expansion of a clump. Tillage spreads the plant. Mulching does not impede this plant in any visible way, unless the mulch is impermeable (black plastic).

35

WILD GARLIC / WILD ONION

Wild Garlic

MORE ABOUT...

I remember picking this weed from my yard as a child and repeatedly smelling and tasting it, even though I was much older when I learned to like the taste of onion or garlic at mealtime. I'm always amused when I show this weed to schoolchildren, because they all say "eeewww!" and then smell it again and hand it to their friends. The strong odor is linked to antibacterial properties of the sulfur-based chemical compounds in onions and their relatives. Perhaps children's love-hate relationship with the smell shows that we are, as humans, drawn to plants that help prevent infection?

CUCKOOFLOWER
(Cardamine pratensis)

Cuckooflower Gone to Seed

DESCRIPTION & LIFE CYCLE

An early spring bloom in the mustard family, often flowering concurrently with daffodils in lawns and gardens. Many-toothed leaves form a rosette, from the center of which rises a stalk with numerous small, white 4-petalled flowers. Seed pods are thin and upright, and will spring loose innumerable miniscule seeds if the plant is disturbed when seeds are ripe. The crazily abundant seed-tossing habit may be the reason for the common name, cuckooflower.

Cuckooflower germinates in fall, survives under snow and through freezing temperatures, and grows additional leaves in early spring. Once flowering time arrives, even the smallest cuckooflower will bloom and set seed, though obviously small ones might set only tens of seeds rather than the hundreds set by larger plants.

BENEFITS

A source of pollen for early insects, including some butterflies. Leaves, flowers and seed pods are edible, with slightly peppery flavor, providing a spring source of greens.

CONTROL

Hand pulling or hoeing, followed by removing plants. However, to be effective, hand removal must take place before seeds are set, because even attempting to remove plants with ripe seeds

CUCKOOFLOWER

will result in wider and uncontrollable seed dispersal. Cuckooflower is not highly competitive, so while it will eagerly cover bare soil, nearby plants are unlikely to be negatively affected. In a lawn, control will be as simple as establishing healthy ground cover (thicker grass, **clover**, and other desirable plants).

MORE ABOUT...

The fact that its flowers are a food source for early insects may be why cuckooflower is thought to be sacred to fairies. If fairies exist, there would be strong evolutionary pressure for them to disguise themselves as insects, so people would be less likely to recognize them for what they are.

This spring, when I picked cuckooflower from our garden beds, I tossed the plants in for our chickens to peck. Since then, I've noticed the chickens seem to seek them out in our yard, so perhaps I've trained our chickens to help me control this plant a bit. I've heard of weeder geese working to control weeds in California, but the problem with using chickens is that they'd just as soon eat the vegetables as the weeds.

Cuckooflower (closeup)

38

DAISIES
English Daisy (Bellis perennis)
Ox-eye Daisy (Leucanthemum vulgare)

Daisies

DESCRIPTION & LIFE CYCLE

Many types of perennial daisies may appear in a lawn (see also **Fleabane**, p. 17). The best suited lawn daisy is the English daisy, a low-growing, short-stemmed plant with a rosette of dark green, egg-shaped leaves at ground level, blooming with 4" – 5" tall, small (1" – 2" in diameter) daisy flowers in early spring, around the time of **dandelion** bloom. Daisy flowers are white to pink, with yellow centers. Ox-eye daisy, which blooms in early summer, is the more classic large-flowered daisy, and its leaves are long and slim, but with toothed edges.

BENEFITS

Daisy flowers are generally attractive, both to humans and to pollinators (particularly bees and beneficial wasps).

CONTROL

English daisy has been cultivated as a lawn species, and there is little reason to control it. Ox-eye daisy will not thrive in lawns, and may be tolerated as a garden plant with little risk of spreading beyond its welcome.

MORE ABOUT...

My daughters and I have enjoyed reading the adventures of Arthur Ransome's young English girl pirates, Nancy and Peggy. In *Swallowdale*, their

DAISIES

great-aunt, whose purpose in life seems to be to squelch their pirate nature, berates their mother in one book for the condition of their lawn, which is thick with English daisies. If I were tempted to believe that the idea of perfect, all-grass lawns were only a North American phenomenon, the character of the great-aunt proves that 1) there have indeed been grass snobs in the past and in other countries as well, and 2) such characters do not make pleasant environments for children, wherever they are. English daisies are featured in Hobbs and Hopkins' seed mix, *Fleur de lawn,* which, though pricey compared to a weedy lawn like mine, is a lovely alternative to the standard lawn. I suspect if Nancy and Peggy's snooty great-aunt heard the name *"Fleur de lawn,"* even she would think whatever plants it contained were worthy in the best neighborhoods.

Ox-eye Daisy (closeup)

Daisy Leaves (young)

GROUND IVY
Creeping Charlie or Creeping Jenny
(Glechoma hederacea)

Ground Ivy

DESCRIPTION & LIFE CYCLE

Ground ivy is a spreading perennial, green in all seasons. Its leaves are paired, rounded and scalloped along a square stem, which roots itself along its path through a lawn or planting bed. Flowers are small (less than ½" long or wide) and lavender, with a larger bottom petal adorned with darker purple streaks. This plant flowers in spring, concurrent with **dandelions** and **violets**.

BENEFITS

Ground ivy is a fine ground cover, with soft leaves to step on, little need for mowing, and a good shot of complementary colors (lavender/green). It provides nectar for early bees, including honeybees and other smaller native bees. It is used medicinally for eye ailments, ringing in the ears, and for clarifying beers as a hops alternative.

CONTROL

This plant spreads easily in a lawn, particularly in shady areas; controlling it in a lawn would require either tillage and reseeding or very regular and strict pruning. Ground ivy also spreads easily from lawn areas into planting beds; garden boundaries (stone, brick, or other low fence, as might be used for a raised bed) can help prevent its spread. Hoeing is not helpful in removing it, because it re-roots itself relatively quickly; hand-pulling would be far more effective. Extremely heavy mulch, or

41

GROUND IVY

Ground Ivy (young)

a layer of newspaper topped with mulch, would kill an existing infestation, but remember that these plants spread rapidly and widely. If you go for the newspaper/mulch solution, follow by hand-pulling around the edge of the mulch, or it will just start right in on colonizing the fresh new surface you've prepared for it.

MORE ABOUT...

Ground ivy or creeping Charlie or creeping Jenny (also sometimes referred to as "gill on the ground"): whatever your name for this plant, you'll find it happiest spreading across a mulched bed. I find this plant does best on shallow topsoil – not necessarily dry areas, but definitely in shade, such as under our overgrown apple tree. Though I haven't used it medicinally, I admire its flowers, and never object to it covering our boring brown mulch under trees with lush, thick growth. No weed whacker or mower necessary.

HEALALL
Self-Heal (Prunella vulgaris)

Healall

DESCRIPTION AND LIFE CYCLE

Heal-all, as it is spelled in Robert Frost's poem *"Design,"* shares with its mint cousins the purple cast it can give a lawn. Healall's top flower petal is often more purple, while the bottom lip of the flower tends to be white, but color variations anywhere between all-white and all-purple are common. Healall leaves are hairless, long and slender (2" – 3" long, ½" – 1" wide), paired opposite one another along the square stem. Flower head is a cylinder about ½ inch thick, with flowers first appearing at the bottom and blooming higher as the early flowers are pollinated and fade. This is a spreading perennial, green in all seasons but blooming and noticeably prettiest in late spring; however, I have seen it in bloom all the way through summer and beyond.

BENEFITS

Attractive and low growing in a lawn, healall is good for bees and other small pollinators. It covers bare ground and remains green in all seasons. Tea brewed from flower heads is said to improve a variety of health conditions, a list too long to repeat here, but with notable claims of improving digestive bacteria, circulation, throat health, liver and bladder function. Leaves are also edible, though noted far more for their health benefits than for any particularly wonderful taste.

43

HEALALL

Healall's name is apt, and though other mints share a great deal with this plant in terms of lawn ecology, few other plants rival it in the number of health claims given to it.

CONTROL

Though there is little reason to want rid of healall entirely, its capacity to overtake a garden patch is notable. In a lawn, even if you should want to check its spread it would probably have to be buried in mulch or fresh topsoil to kill it. In a garden, regular hand-pulling of the patch edges may be needed. If pulled in wet weather, remove plants from site or they may re-root themselves rather than die.

MORE ABOUT...

Given how easily it grows, it is a wonder that pharmaceutical companies are able to compete with it – but of course, pharmaceutical companies have a much higher advertising budget.

Healall (closeup)

Healall (young)

44

HENBIT/PURPLE DEADNETTLE
Henbit (Lamium amplexicaule)
Purple Deadnettle (Lamium purpureum)

Henbit

DESCRIPTION & LIFE CYCLE

Both henbit and purple deadnettle are annual members of the mint family (square-stemmed), germinating in fall and flowering in spring; both die back in the heat of summer, after setting seed. Leaves have scalloped edges and are hairy, though hairs are only visible with help from strong reading glasses. Flowers are similar to **ground ivy** (small, purple, tube-shaped with a showy lower "lip" on the flower) if you look close enough to see them. Henbit leaves clasp the stem and are somewhat heart-shaped, while purple deadnettle leaves are almost triangular. Purple deadnettle is named not for the flower color (which is purple) but for the purplish tint to the tips of the flowering stalks.

BENEFITS

Since these annuals are relatively small plants and germinate best on bare soil, they can act as a free cover crop, preventing erosion in field crops during the barren winter months and before spring planting. They are low growing and provide good added color. The leaves of both are edible, though the hairiness can be a bit off-putting for some. Both plants have some reported medicinal uses, one of which is to reduce bleeding, and another is to induce sweating – perhaps useful

45

HENBIT

Henbit (closeup)

for wrestlers and other people with steroid-induced swelling? Their flowers are attractive to honeybees and other small native pollinators.

CONTROL

Because they germinate best on bare soil, the best prevention is providing good ground cover. In a flowerbed, a thick layer of mulch in fall would probably prevent germination; in a lawn, sowing **clover** or grass in early fall (an excellent practice for any lawn) would help reduce available bare patches and help out-compete the mint seedlings.

These annual mints grow a bit taller than **ground ivy** and don't cover the ground year-round, making them less desirable as lawn cover. However, controlling henbit and deadnettle is easier than controlling ground ivy. Many lawns look better with a bit more purple in spring, whether from violets or mints, and a thoroughly infested lawn is a welcome antidote to the browns and whites and grays of winter.

Purple Deadnettle

CREEPING VERONICA
Common Speedwell (Veronica officinalis)

Creeping Veronica (closeup)

DESCRIPTION & LIFE CYCLE

Creeping veronica has tiny, slightly fuzzy oval or somewhat triangular leaves, in pairs lying opposite each other along a low-growing, spreading stem. Flowers are purple or blue, with 4 petals, one deeply colored at the bottom of the flower, and one smaller, lighter-colored petal at the top. Foliage is light green in color, and flowers are strikingly attractive – well worth examining up close. In a lawn, you will often find them growing in clumps.

This is a low-growing perennial plant, adding a light-green note to patches of sunny turf. Seeds and seed heads are not noticeable or at all unattractive. Creeping veronica flowers much of the summer, but mostly in spring, beginning when the **dandelions** flower.

BENEFITS

Its flowers are attractive to beneficial insects. The foliage has medicinal properties, helping with coughs and skin ailments. This plant is not reported to be edible. The fact that it is low-growing and perennial makes it a welcome addition to lawns.

CREEPING VERONICA

Creeping Veronica

CONTROL

Creeping veronica can be dug or pulled fairly easily, and is slow growing. It does not tend to invade garden beds. Mulching will suppress it, but pulling is recommended first, to weaken the plant before letting mulch finish the job.

MORE ABOUT...

Creeping veronica blooms do not make good cut flowers in the usual sense, because their stems are so small, but gathering a handful of flowering stems will give you a bouquet that can look lovely for a day or two in a glass. Sometimes, my daughters will pick a variety of small flowers, with creeping veronica, **cinquefoil**, **henbit**, **wild garlic**, **bluets** and **violets** – all without stems – and these can be placed in a small white bowl of water and set on the table, looking quite pretty for several hours or a day.

BUTTERCUP
Many species (Ranunculus spp.)

Buttercup

DESCRIPTION

Buttercup leaves generally have 3 to 5 main lobes with a deep points along the edge of each. Leaves are typically low on the ground, though the plant will grow up onto shrubs, almost like a vine. Flowers are distinctively shiny, buttery yellow, and centers have lots of yellow anthers, bearing pollen.

BENEFITS

The shiny, yellow center is highly attractive to bees, as well as people; grows well in damp, semi-shaded areas.

CONTROL

This plant is toxic to horses and other grazers – fortunately they usually stop eating before it kills them. However, because they won't eat it, buttercup spreads in pastures. In lawns, pulling it regularly will suppress it, if you're worried about spread into a neighboring area.

MORE ABOUT...

Sheila remembers using this plant as a sort of childhood makeup, rubbing it on her cheeks to add some yellow color. The flowers can be relatively large and showy, compared to many weeds.

49

WILD STRAWBERRY
(Potentilla simplex)

Wild Strawberry (flowers and fruit)

DESCRIPTION

Wild strawberry is a very low-growing plant, with 5-parted tooth-edged leaves, alternating along the stem, which twines across the ground. Flowers, which appear concurrent with the main flush of dandelion flowers, are the same brilliant yellow as dandelions, but are less than dime-sized, and have 5 petals. Similar plants in the same genus (Potentilla) may grow taller, so a homeowner who recognizes it may see its siblings in natural areas.

LIFE CYCLE

Its attractive and ornate foliage is present year-round. Yellow flowers appear in spring to early summer. Small, red "wild strawberries" develop in midsummer, and are beloved by birds and small mammals but are not tasty or sweet like domestic strawberry.

BENEFITS

Leaves and flowers are edible, and may be eaten directly, or made into tea or other tonics to improve skin and digestion. Small bees and other early beneficial insects use this very low-growing flower for pollen and nectar. *Note:* The viney stems may sneak into garden beds. If so, frequent pulling or pruning may be needed to prevent an invasion from becoming well established.

CHICKWEED
Common (Stellaria media)
Mouseear (Cerastium fontanum)

Chickweed

DESCRIPTION & LIFE CYCLE

This is a low-growing winter annual, germinating in fall and flowering in spring, as trees begin to leaf out. Leaves are arranged in pairs along twining green stems. Small (½" in diameter), white flowers, with what look like 10 petals but are really 5 petals, each split almost or entirely in two. Common chickweed leaves are pointed at the tip, smooth and slightly shiny; mouseear chickweed leaves, as the name implies, are slightly fuzzy, and more rounded at the tip.

BENEFITS

Because it flowers and dies in early spring, chickweed typically does not compete with vegetable or flower gardens. Chickweed is edible in spring salads. The plant is not strongly flavored, though common chickweed may be preferable, since mouseear leaves' fuzzy texture may be off-putting. It is reported to be medicinal for skin ailments.

Chickweed can be of great benefit to the soil, both in gardens and on farms. Chickweed often volunteers in crop fields left unplowed in fall, providing soil cover – preventing erosion – during the winter months. Though farmers typically do not plant it for this purpose, a good chickweed infestation may actually save soil and help prevent nutrient runoff in winter. In a garden or lawn,

51

CHICKWEED

Chickweed

chickweed can serve the same purpose during winter – helping prevent erosion, capture carbon dioxide, and maintain soil nutrients.

CONTROL

Chickweed can reproduce abundantly, so if allowed to go to seed in a flower bed, the area affected will certainly be larger next year. Control involves mulching or hand-weeding, best done in fall or early winter, when plants are at their smallest. Mulch may require a layer of newspaper underneath if the plant is being controlled in spring, when it is at its strongest. Chickweed germinates best in areas with no other plants – it is not a vigorous competitor – so if present in a lawn, it can be reduced by over-seeding bare areas with desirable perennial plants (see **clover**).

Chickweed

DANDELION
(Taraxacum officinale)

Dandelion

DESCRIPTION AND LIFE CYCLE

Leaves in a perennial rosette, varying from slightly ragged-edged to having deep, saw-like teeth. Flowers are large and brilliantly yellow, with fluffy, round, white seed heads that are irresistible to children, but considered unattractive to many homeowners (fairly or unfairly). Flowers wilt quickly once picked. Dandelion is a perennial, with leaves and roots present in all seasons. It flowers abundantly in spring, as tulips begin flowering, but may flower in any month.

BENEFITS

Dandelion roots may be dried, ground, and made into a coffee substitute. The leaves are a nutritious spring green (becoming more bitter later in the season; though still edible, cooking improves them by reducing bitterness). Dandelion flowers may be gathered and brewed into a brandy-like wine, which can be drunk medicinally or recreationally. Sap from dandelion flower stems may be used in treating skin ailments. Dandelion is an excellent source of nectar and pollen for beneficial insects, including honeybees.

CONTROL

Young dandelions are easily removed by hand, while adult dandelions, with their deep taproot, must be removed with a forked dandelion prong.

53

DANDELION

Depending on the condition of the lawn and the size of the dandelion, a homeowner may wish to seed ground cover (grass and **clover**) after pulling the plant, because the remaining bare patch is a prime location for re-growth of the injured dandelion or for germination of a new one. Young dandelions are not very competitive with healthy turf, primarily germinating in locations where grass is weak. Mowing too close (under 3") will weaken grass roots, expose more bare soil, and facilitate dandelion growth and germination.

MORE ABOUT...

Young humans, like dandelion flowers, are far more attractive than older humans. When we are choosing our spouses, we rarely consider what they will look like when they go to seed (for more information, see your parents-in-law). I think it is unfair that with dandelions some people fail to see the beauty of their youth simply because they know the plant will be less attractive a couple of weeks later.

*Dandelion
(seed head)*

*Dandelion
(various stages)*

Dandelion (young greens)

BLUET
(Houstonia caerulea)

Bluet

DESCRIPTION & LIFE CYCLE

This low-growing perennial plant may grow either in clusters (common in lawns) or singly (common in woodlands). Small (just under ½" in diameter) sky-blue flowers with yellow centers, 4 petals. Leaves are light green, oval, slightly pointed at the tip, and form a small rosette at ground level, with one pair of leaves an inch or two below the bloom. Bluet is native to eastern North America and blooms for a couple of weeks to a month, as first **dandelion** flush is going to seed.

BENEFITS

This plant is so pretty it is worthwhile to mow around it if you're lucky enough to have it. Grows on rocky, thin soil but also thrives in some lawns. Not aggressively spreading. When the flowers die back and the plant goes to seed, the plant is so tiny as to be hardly noticeable, but the space remains green, year-round. Most of all, it is just simply lovely.

CONTROL

Why would you want to? Hand-pulling or hoeing would easily kill it, if it were, unimaginably, growing in a place where it wasn't wanted. Transplanting would be worthwhile – unappreciative hosts of bluet should consider giving the plant as a gift.

BLUET

Bluet (closeup)

MORE ABOUT...

Putting this plant in a weed ID guide may be cheating, for the plant would almost never be considered a weed, either by a naturalist or a gardener. However, it is a volunteer in my lawn and in many other healthy, semi-wild lawns. If my lawn were treated, the bluets would die, even if no one ever called them an infestation. I consider bluet to be the best symbol of what lovely plants may be unknowingly lost if we "treat" our lawns for weeds. Who knows what surprises will grow and flower for us in our lawns, if we give them a bit of a chance?

VIOLET
(Viola sororia)

DESCRIPTION & LIFE CYCLE

Deep green, spade-shaped leaves with low-growing, spreading habit. Violet flowers have five petals and typically are purple, ranging from white to almost blue, though some related types of wild violets are also yellow; color combinations are also common. Prefers growing in shade or partial shade. Violet is a perennial, with leaves attractive and green in all seasons. It flowers most abundantly in spring, concurrent with daffodils and tulips, but may flower from early spring to late fall.

BENEFITS

Violet flowers are edible, and are a pretty addition to any salad, or may be made into candied flowers. The lovely, shy flowers last a bit longer than **dandelions**, once picked, and are worth putting in a small vase for a day or two.

Violet (closeup)

They produce unnoticeable seeds. The plant has no life stage that is unattractive.

CONTROL

I cannot imagine any reason why violets would need to be controlled in a lawn, as they require no mowing, fill shady spaces that might otherwise have limited ground cover, and offer such richly beautiful flowers. In a flowerbed, they can be reduced in number by digging them out, though their roots are often strongly held to the ground and also disperse; it would be hard to dig out

57

VIOLET

a violet without doing damage to nearby plants. Violets are not strong competitors with other garden plants, and they do not spread quickly (by roots, stems, or seeds), so even in a vegetable or flower garden I would recommend tolerance rather than elimination as a successful strategy.

MORE ABOUT...

Even now, as a boring adult, I like to get down at ground level where violets are blooming, and lose my troubles for a moment in their soothing colors. One day I was lying in the lawn with our violets, and our neighbor came to ask if I'd fallen or was hurt. I wasn't hurt, and I appreciated their worry for me as kind-hearted, though I do wish it were more usual and normal for grown people to immerse themselves in the color and variety of their lawns.

Violet

58

YELLOW ROCKET
Spring Rocket (Barbarea vulgaris)

Yellow Rocket

DESCRIPTION AND LIFE CYCLE

Briefly, yellow rocket looks like wild broccoli. In spring, a fall-germinating rosette of deep-green leaves with irregular, scalloped, oblong leaves shoots up, first to a few branches of broccoli-like flower heads (roughly concurrent with **dandelions**), and later to a cluster of golden yellow, 4-petalled flowers, each roughly ¼" – ½" in diameter. The flowers themselves are like yellow versions of **garlic mustard** or **cuckooflower**. The seed heads resemble super-skinny beans pointing skyward (similar to seed heads of garlic mustar**d** and cuckooflower) – green at first, then maturing to a dry tan. When dry, seed heads will seem to explode on contact.

BENEFITS

Edible and nutritious, like broccoli. Though the flavor is stronger than domestic broccoli, cooking and flavoring can make its flavor more mild. Most children will try this plant, but usually will recoil at the bitterness. It is, however, easily palatable, even delicious, in **Spring Greens Quiche** (see recipe on p.87). As an intangible benefit, its flower color is the kind of yellow we seem to instinctively crave after the gray and brown of early spring.

59

YELLOW ROCKET

CONTROL

Yellow rocket will not generally flower if its stem is mowed even once, so mowing is generally sufficient to suppress it from rising above the lawn. It produces prolific and long-lived seeds, so if it grows in a garden, it can be tolerated for food or flowers, but flower heads should be picked before seed set, unless you'd like to grow it next spring on a much larger scale.

There are a number of weedy members of this family, all of them edible. Though yellow rocket is the one that most dramatically resembles broccoli, greens from any mustard, fall or spring, are safely edible. I have occasionally mowed around it, even in my front yard, to let it go to flower, depending on how rebellious I feel at the moment about the constraints of suburban life.

Yellow Rocket (young greens)

Yellow Rocket (closeup)

WOOD SORREL
(Oxalis acetosella)

Wood Sorrel

DESCRIPTION & LIFE CYCLE

A summer annual, germinating in early spring. Leaves are light green, 3-parted and closely resemble **clover**, except wood sorrel's leaf tips are heart-shaped (indented at the tip) instead of rounded. Flowers are yellow, slightly bell-shaped and bearing 5 petals. Seed heads are bean-like, roughly ½" long, and explode when touched at peak ripeness, guaranteeing a fresh supply of wood sorrel next spring. This plant will sometimes germinate in fall and survive winter, though when it does the leaf color tends to be reddish or purplish; I don't know if this is a stress response or a natural antifreeze.

BENEFITS

Though many plants are edible, this is one of the few that I find children tend to like at first taste. The mild, sour flavor is really lovely and the leaf texture is delicate.

CONTROL

Since this plant is an annual, its presence in lawns indicates that bare patches could have been seeded in fall or earlier in spring. Wood sorrel is not very competitive, in the sense that it will not germinate or thrive in the dense vegetation of healthy lawn cover. However, it is short-lived, and in a lawn is not worth pulling, because the solution to it is to re-seed bare patches (I simply walk around in fall, about the time of first frost, and scatter grass or clover seed, without adding

WOOD SORREL

Wood Sorrel (closeup)

soil). In a garden, this plant must be hand pulled, unless you want the population to increase dramatically. Fresh layers of mulch in early spring (before it germinates) will also work well to suppress it, since the seeds germinate best from the soil surface where they landed after springing from last year's plants.

MORE ABOUT...

My mom called this plant "sourgrass." Though this is clearly not a grass, it is sour-tasting, and it was the only edible weed my mom told me about – I tasted it often. Later, when I was in college, I house-sat for my botany professor, and was instructed to weed this one regularly, with the phrase "One year's seeding is nine year's weeding." The flavor, given by oxalic acid, is chemically the same as the flavor of rhubarb.

BIRDSFOOT TREFOIL
(Lotus corniculatus)

Birdsfoot Trefoil

DESCRIPTION & LIFE CYCLE

Birdsfoot trefoil is a perennial legume, with triple leaflets, green year-round – like **clover**. Unlike clover, birdsfoot trefoil has a taproot and does not spread; it can grow tall and lanky in pasture, though its stem is not strong. Flowers of birdsfoot trefoil are brilliant yellow, growing in clusters at stem tops, with a single rounded petal on top, and lower petals meeting to form a pocket, in the classic pea-flower form. Flowering continues throughout summer.

BENEFITS

As a legume, birdsfoot trefoil fixes nitrogen and helps enrich soil; the taproot may also serve to loosen compacted soils. This plant has an attractive foliage and flowers. Birdsfoot trefoil grows well in dry conditions, such as along roadsides, and in poor soils with high acidity. Remarkably, however, it can also tolerate periods of flooding.

CONTROL

This plant does not easily tolerate low mowing, so its presence is probably an indication that the lawn is tending toward meadow height. Lower and more regular mowing will reduce its presence in a lawn.

BIRDSFOOT TREFOIL

MORE ABOUT...

Birdsfoot trefoil is not typically considered a weed by farmers, who view it as a pasture plant, an excellent source of protein for grazing animals, especially on poor land where alfalfa cannot thrive. However, since taller lawns are more sensible from an energy perspective, its presence indicates that the lawn owner is doing something really right, even if the soil is too poor to be well suited for gardening.

Birdsfoot Trefoil (closeup)

Birdsfoot Trefoil with Foliage

BLACK MEDIC
(Medicago lupulina)

Black Medic (closeup)

DESCRIPTION & LIFE CYCLE

Closely related and very similar to **clover**. Leaves are 3-parted, with each part oval. This low-growing plant is an annual in northern climates – not generally present in winter – making it slightly less desirable in lawns, but it may overwinter and appear again if weather isn't too harsh. Flowers bloom in early summer, around the time **wood sorrel** blooms and the dogwood trees have mostly faded. Flowers are yellow balls, smaller than clover (¼" diameter) but similar in shape.

How it is different from clover: Clover leaves each have a whitish mark or stripe around the center of each leaf; black medic lacks this, and has slightly deeper-green leaves overall. Black medic plants are more clearly individuals – if you pull up a black medic, you can get a whole plant, separate from its neighbors – while clover plants tend to blend and tangle so that separating one plant from another in a lawn is nearly impossible.

BENEFITS

This is a nitrogen-fixing plant. Its presence may indicate that your lawn has bare patches, compacted soil, or low nutrients, and it helps resolve these problems by adding nitrogen and loosening the soil a bit. Like clover, black medic is attractive to bees and other small pollinators, though its flowers are a bit small to be easily accessible food for honeybees (this is good if you're worried about stinging bees, but bad if you are hoping for maximum honey production).

BLACK MEDIC

Black Medic

CONTROL

In a lawn, pulling it would be silly, but reseeding with other plants will help reduce it. Black medic tends to grow best at edges, and often is the best-quality ground cover that will grow easily in these spots. I recommend pulling it only from garden beds.

In my neighborhood, black medic grows thick around the edge of the gravel track at the elementary school, in the demilitarized zone between pure lawn and pure gravel. It tolerates traffic, and has the audacity, seemingly, to try to grow in soil with almost no nutrients. It tolerates close mowing and moderate shade. Black medic definitely has my respect as a plant living its life relatively harmlessly in tough spots.

CLOVER
**Dutch White (Trifolium repens);
Alsike (T. hybridum); Red (T. pratense)**

Clover Foliage

Clover (closeup)

DESCRIPTION & LIFE CYCLE

Clover is a low-growing, deep green perennial with 3 leaflets, each oval/round at the tip, and with a slightly gray/white band of color running across all leaflets in an arc. Flowers are a ball of small white/pink tubes (each of which is actually a small floret in its own right). **Wood sorrel** can be easily confused for clover, but the tips of sorrel leaves are dented (heart-shaped), and sorrel is typically a lighter green. (Note: shamrocks are actually related to wood sorrel, not clover.) Clover flowers in summer, but its leaves provide ground cover in all four seasons.

BENEFITS

This plant contributes nitrogen to soil through a symbiosis with bacteria living in its root nodules. It requires little mowing, except as desired to cut blooms, but one of the great advantages of clover is its attraction for honeybees. Clover is not vulnerable to lawn grubs, as grass is. A mixture of clover and grass in a lawn requires less fertilizer and pest control than an all-grass lawn.

CONTROL

Though I see no reason to control clover in a lawn, newspaper topped with mulch, kept in place for a warm season, would squelch an existing patch. A small area could be controlled with hand weeding, but it would be difficult to pull clover without pulling other plants in the area.

CLOVER

MORE ABOUT...

Many of us in childhood tasted honeysuckle nectar by gently pulling the flower out from its stem and sucking on the base – getting just an instant sense of sweetness on the tongue. Red clover, the larger species most commonly grown in pastures, can give this same experience. I remember tasting red clover nectar for the first time during recess in elementary school, when a friend showed me how to pull the flowers gently out. Unfortunately, at my daughters' school, even white clover is not tolerated due to fear of bee stings and lawsuits. Red clover is a taller plant, and standard lawns are too short for it, but if a lawn were kept at 6" – 10" – more like a meadow – red clover could be seeded and cultivated.

Alsike Clover – Tolerant of Wet Soil

MOSS
(many possible species)

DESCRIPTION & LIFE CYCLE

Moss is a low-growing (½" to a few inches) evergreen ground cover that does not produce a flower. Of the variable forms of moss, most have green stems covered by tiny green leaves. Moss has a complex life cycle, with the green, most commonly seen plant being haploid (one set of chromosomes) and only the seed head being the standard diploid (two sets), like most plants. Moss is usually seen in patches, from a few inches in diameter to several yards wide. No matter how large the patches get, it is actually very slow-growing. Strongly prefers moist soils. Though moss does grow well on north faces of trees or houses due to the relative lack of drying sunshine, it can grow on any side, so moss cannot reliably be used for way-finding in forests.

Moss

BENEFITS

Moss is soft on bare feet and does not require mowing. It is green year-round, and most vivid in warmer months. It can be transplanted, but be advised, its need for constant moisture results in many transplanted patches dying of dehydration. Moss can be used on "green" roofs to reduce urban storm water runoff, thereby improving water quality.

MOSS

CONTROL

Standard household vinegar kills moss quite easily, though it also kills other lawn plants. I discovered this while using vinegar to clean algal growth off our house siding, and the mossy spot where I kept the bucket of vinegar and rinsed my washcloths remains brown and dead, now about 8 months later. Moss is not highly competitive, however, and there are few situations where control is warranted – besides perhaps on roofs or siding, where it holds moisture and can contribute to wood rot.

MORE ABOUT...

Something for the children: In the novel *Kate Vaiden*, by Reynolds Price, Kate's mother shows her how to make a magical-looking moss garden by digging a hole, lining it with moss and putting flowers inside, then covering the hole with a small piece of glass. Another patch of moss may be used to hide the "Penny Show" until the requisite coin has been produced.

Moss

Moss and Lichen on Tree Bark

70

PLANTAIN
Toe-knockers
(Plantago major, Plantago lanceolata)

Plantain

DESCRIPTION & LIFE CYCLE

The perennial plantain leaves grow in a rosette. For broadleaf plantain *(P. major)*, leaves are almost egg-xactly egg-sized and -shaped; for buckhorn plantain *(P. lanceolata)* they're more strappy and slender. Both leaves have very tough veins, and if the leaf is pulled apart, veins may seem to be like fibrous strings. The plant sends up a flower stalk in midsummer, with either a pipe-cleaner-like fuzzy flower along the top 2" to 4" of broadleaf plantain's flower stalk *(P. major)* or a tufted fingernail-sized ball topping the buckhorn stalk *(P. lanceolata)*. Though the flower stalk can look rangy and tall in a lawn, the leaves themselves remain low-growing.

BENEFITS

Grows in compacted and/or damp soils, providing year-round green cover where many other plants fail to thrive. Buckhorn plantain's flower stalk can provide entertaining play for children of all ages, as it can be twisted around the finger and shot with a catapult action. Leaves are edible in salad (though the veins' stringiness may make them more appealing cooked), and the plant can be used medicinally as a treatment for skin ailments, and is said to reduce nicotine cravings.

71

PLANTAIN

Plantain Foliage   **Plantain Heads**

CONTROL

Incredibly difficult to pull from lawns, especially since its tough, fibrous roots cling particularly well in the compacted soil it tends to grow best in. Control is best accomplished by soil aeration and by controlling traffic patterns. Plantain grows most abundantly in the most heavily trafficked areas of a lawn; stepping stones may be used to change foot traffic, while aeration and composting are doing their work to encourage growth of more desirable species. In a garden, plantain can be hand-pulled or smothered by a layer of newspaper (topped with fresh soil or compost) or simply with thick mulch. It prefers full sun, so increased shade can also reduce it, though this will do little to solve the soil compaction problem, which plantain is doing its best to tell you about.

MORE ABOUT...

In our own lawn, plantain grows quite thick around the south-facing corner of the house where we walk en route to tend the chickens. I don't mind it so much. It keeps the area from eroding, and it isn't hard to mow. I actually really like watching the plantain heads fly up like popcorn in front of my reel mower.

PURSLANE
(Portulaca olereacea)

Purslane (young)

DESCRIPTION & LIFE CYCLE

This flat-growing plant has succulent, thick leaves, usually roughly an inch long, and a thick stem. Purslane grows best in dry places (sand, gravel), but will also grow in gardens. Purslane leaves are deep green, slightly shiny, with small whitish hairs underneath. The leaf edges and stems often have a purplish or reddish cast, depending on the nutrient status of the soil. Flowers are close along the stem and are nondescript. The plant is annual, germinating around the time of **clover** flowering. It dies at first frost.

Nutritional benefits include omega-3 fatty acids, high beta-carotene, and good levels of magnesium and potassium. Good for blood pressure and cholesterol.

BENEFITS

Purslane leaves are edible, with a satisfying crunchy texture at first bite, juicy/slimy inside, and slightly sour taste (similar to **wood sorrel**).

CONTROL

It is easily pulled, but so nutritious that pulling the plant should probably wait until you're ready to start cooking.

73

PURSLANE

MORE ABOUT...

Featured in the *New York Times* food section in 2006 and 2009, this plant is beloved in many cultures. Purslane may be used in soups (substitute for celery, or okra) and salads (especially good with feta and good black olives). My neighbor, Tanyel Turkaslan-Bulbul, is originally from Turkey. She had cooked with the plant growing up and considers it a delicacy, and she was thrilled to learn that it was growing in our own neighborhood. (See Tanyel's recipe for **Yogurt & Purslane Salad** on p.89.)

Purslane (closeup)

Purslane Sprouts

QUEEN ANNE'S LACE
Wild Carrot (Daucus carota)

Queen Anne's Lace

DESCRIPTION & LIFE CYCLE

Queen Anne's lace has feathery, ornate leaves on a hairy (unlike **poison hemloc**k or **yarrow**) stem, which begin as a rosette in year one, with a flowering stalk arising in the plant's second year. Flower heads are flat and white (sometimes pale pink), with a single, tiny dark-violet flower somewhere in the center of the spray of white. Plant spreads and rises to roughly 1 to 2 feet tall while flowering. Plant smells strongly like carrots. Seed heads curl into themselves and merit another of the plant's common names, *"Bird's nest."* Seeds have sticky hairs on the outside.

BENEFITS

Flowers are a good source of food for a number of small wasps and other beneficial pollinators. Leaves are an important food source for some swallowtail butterflies, including the black swallowtail. At the end of the first year, before it makes a flowering stalk, the root is a good substitute for carrot, a close cousin.

CONTROL

Typically will not invade lawns, because close mowing does not allow it to reproduce there. In a garden, pulling (with a dandelion prong) at the end of year one will prove easier than pulling in year two. As the plant goes to seed, pulling is pointless because the plant is at the end of its life. Gloves may be worn when pulling, because extensive contact with the leaves can cause skin to be photosensitive.

YARROW
Milfoil (Achillea millefolium)

Yarrow (closeup)

DESCRIPTION & LIFE CYCLE

Yarrow has feathery, ornate leaves that begin as a rosette, with a flowering stalk emerging from mature plants – similar to **Queen Anne's lace**. Yarrow leaves are not hairy, though. Flowers throughout summer, typically from a single stalk, in a flat array of small (¼" – ½" diameter), separate pink-white daisy-shaped blooms.

BENEFITS

Flowers are excellent for pollinators. However, in a lawn, where flower stalks rarely get a chance to rise above mower height, yarrow's best feature is its feathery, delicate foliage.

CONTROL

Unlike Queen Anne's lace, yarrow will persist in a lawn, even when it is not allowed to flower, so mowing will not eliminate it. I can't imagine wanting to remove it from a flower bed (transplant to a better site, if desired), or especially from a lawn.

RED SORREL
(Rumex acetosa)

Red Sorrel

DESCRIPTION & LIFE CYCLE

Leaves of this plant can be quite distinctive, with a long, rounded tip, narrowing at the base before flaring out into matching slender points, perpendicular to the leaf mid-vein. On younger plants, leaves can also be simply long and slender (with a bit of a square base). The plant begins as an individual cluster of leaves – not so organized as a rosette – but will send runners, like a strawberry plant; a single plant may gradually cover a fairly large area. Stems and veins are often red, giving the plant a color resemblance to rhubarb, its flavor cousin. Flowers are individually nondescript, but the collection of them looks more like a loose spray of small red buds rather than the fully-expanded flowers that they are. Grows particularly well in wet soils and mulched areas.

BENEFITS

Attractive at times, good ground cover, and edible. Oxalic acid gives red sorrel its distinctive sour taste, like its cousin rhubarb and the unrelated **wood sorrel** *(Oxalis)*. This also means raw sorrel should not be eaten in excess. Excess is not overly dangerous – just stomach discomfort – and really, how many of us actually eat too many greens?

RED SORREL

Red Sorrel (young and most edible)

CONTROL

In a lawn, though the plant can look quite attractive in flower, dried seed heads can look untidy, but mowing can easily solve this. The plant is best pulled by hand to remove the roots. If eaten regularly through the winter (the plant retains its leaves year-round) little further control may be needed by spring.

Red sorrel had completely taken over the area under our backyard swing set over the last few years, because I like its flowers and I did nothing to slow it. I did eventually discover that it gets stuck between my bare toes in August, however, so I decided this year to feed it to the chickens. Whenever the snow retreated this winter, I pulled red sorrel clumps and piled them up in the coop for our chickens, who didn't ask me to clean and separate the leaves from the roots as I would have to do in cooking for humans.

SCARLET PIMPERNEL
Poor man's weatherglass
(Anagallis arvensis)

Scarlet Pimpernel

DESCRIPTION & LIFE CYCLE

This diminutive cousin of the primrose might first appear to be a new patch of common **chickweed**: pairs of hairless, simple, small (½") leaves lie opposite one another along twining, delicate green stems. However, chickweed blooms around the time pimpernel begins its life each year, and by the time scarlet pimpernel is busy forecasting summer thunderstorms (see below), chickweed is generally long gone. The flowers of scarlet pimpernel, however, are unmistakable: five petals the light red of a cardinal feather held up to sunlight, tiny yellow anthers sending pollen from the flower's center, and the tiniest lavender center – only for the observer who bothers to look closely. Blooms in mid-summer. Its flowers close up with the darkening skies of incoming storms, hence its other common name.

BENEFITS

Small flowers probably good for some very small pollinators. Aesthetic benefit: just plain lovely. Its colors are every bit as beautiful as the most gaudy of pansies, and getting a weather forecast from it is an extra bonus.

CONTROL

This plant is not at all competitive, and tends to grow in places with at least partial direct sun exposure and few other plants. If you have

SCARLET PIMPERNEL

scarlet pimpernel and you really don't want it, plant something else larger or more vigorous, and the pimpernel will probably fail to return to your garden. I am sure that the flower fairies will then find someone else who appreciates it more, next summer.

MORE ABOUT...

It is probably not fair for me to put this plant in a book of common lawn weeds, because it isn't really all that common. However, I think of scarlet pimpernel as one of the best little surprises that might visit people who don't spray their mulch beds, who don't compulsively weed near their buildings, and who pay attention to details outdoors. Because it is toxic to grazing animals (who are generally smart enough to avoid it), it would probably be a great deer-resistant annual if someone bred it to be a bit larger.

Scarlet Pimpernel (closeup)

Scarlet Pimpernel – Seed Pod

HORSETAIL
Field horsetail, Common horsetail, Bottlebrush, Horsetail fern (Equisetum arvense)

Horsetail

DESCRIPTION & LIFE CYCLE

At first glance, horsetail looks like a spindly grass – it grows to 6" – 8" high, leaves are thin, and flowers are totally nondescript when they're present at all. In spring, fertile stems look a bit like **buckhorn plantain** flowering stalks and a bit like pale asparagus. After fertile stems have died back, vegetative stalks arise, and are round, with thin, round leaves/stems arising in whorls from nodes every inch or so up the stalk. Horsetail does well on poor soils – either sandy soils, or poorly drained soils – and is resistant to most herbicides. In the wild, it is often seen growing near pond or stream banks. It dies back in autumn.

BENEFITS

Horsetail does have some medicinal properties, including as a diuretic and topical wound treatment. It also may increase bone calcium. However, poisoning is possible (children have been poisoned by using the hollow stems of horsetail as whistles), so I do not recommend home preparation.

CONTROL

As this plant is not highly competitive, most perennial ground covers are capable of growing over horsetail. Increasing soil organic matter (adding compost) would also help decrease

HORSETAIL

horsetail by increasing competition from other plants. It will easily grow through mulch, but a barrier such as newspaper should also work.

MORE ABOUT...

This genus, *Equisetum*, is one of the remaining dinosaur-era plants. It is not truly a flowering plant in the modern sense, but an ancient line of plants which had relatives growing like small trees, 15 feet tall. Fossils of this plant can be found in many parts of the U.S. and Canada, and plants may have incredibly long life spans. I have a lot of respect for *Equisetum*, because of its long and successful history. Sometimes I see this plant as I am walking along streams, great blue herons flying overhead, and feel like I can imagine what the world was like millions of years ago.

Horsetail (closeup)

LADY'S THUMB
Lady's Thumb (Persicaria vulgaris)
Pennsylvania smartweed
(Polygonum pennsylvanicum)

Lady's Thumb

DESCRIPTION & LIFE CYCLE

These close cousins, both annuals, have white or pink flower clusters along stem tips; each flower looks like a small ball (roughly ⅛" diameter) and never appears to open past bud stage. Leaves are slender and pointed, about 3" – 6" long and about 1" wide, with a darker splotch in the center. At the base of the leaf, clasping the stem, both plants have a thin sheath (this sheath has long hairs or bristles for lady's thumb but is bare for smartweed). If you want to distinguish the two, remember that this lady has a hairy thumb. Both prefer damp soil and tolerate shade. Flowers in mid- to late summer. Before flowering, leaves look similar to **dayflower**, though dayflower leaves lack the dark splotch in the center and also lack the sheath around the leaf base.

BENEFITS

Unusual among weeds for its pink flower color. Flowers provide nectar for beneficial wasps and small bees.

CONTROL

This plant is common around lawn edges, where you're more likely to be weed-whacking than mowing. Control can be accomplished with closer mowing or more frequent cutting.

83

DAYFLOWER
(Commelina communis)

Dayflower

DESCRIPTION & LIFE CYCLE

Foliage of dayflower looks very much like a very wide-bladed (just under 1") spreading grass, or perhaps a lily. Grass-like leaves alternate along flexible green stems. Dayflower tends to form a mound by mid to late summer. Brilliant blue, asymmetrical 2-petalled flowers with sunny yellow stamens open in midsummer (the small white petal beneath is visible only for those who examine closely). It got the name dayflower because each flower lasts a single day. This plant is an annual that grows in the heat of summer only, but typically in part or full shade.

BENEFITS

Beauty. Originally cultivated as a garden flower, it was introduced from Asia. The leaves and flowers are edible raw (salads) or dried in tea. Its texture also survives brief stir-frying. Dayflower has some medicinal use, in part as an anti-inflammatory.

CONTROL

Easy to pull in a garden, or to mow down at the edge of a lawn. Spreads by seed, so if one year's infestation is particularly bad, newspaper and mulch can help prevent germination the following summer.

Garlic Mustard Colcannon

2 pounds potatoes
3 – 4 cups garlic mustard leaves (if not enough available, substitute kale for some garlic mustard)
1/8 – 1/4 cup butter or olive oil
1/2 sweet onion
Salt and pepper to taste

Boil and mash potatoes. Sauté onion in butter/oil until slightly browned. Add garlic mustard to pan, cooking until color brightens. Add mashed potatoes and heat through.

Serve hot. Also good with ham or bacon added.

Serves 8 as a side dish, 4 as a main dish

Garlic mustard greens can be found in most seasons, excluding only mid-summer, when old stalks are dead and new plants just germinating. Greens tend to be least bitter when young (fall, winter and early spring).

Spring Greens Quiche

3 – 4 eggs
1/2 cup half-and-half (optional – makes quiche lighter/creamier, but also much less healthy)
2 cups shredded cheese (Swiss, mozzarella especially)
1/4 cup parmesan cheese
2 – 3 cups spring greens from among the following: wild onion, wild garlic, yellow rocket leaves or green flower heads (broccoli stage), dandelion greens, red sorrel leaves
1 tsp. sea salt
1/2 tsp. nutmeg may be added to cut bitterness of greens if desired
Pie crust

Preheat oven to 375°F (191°C). Chop greens together. Combine eggs, half-and-half, cheese, salt and nutmeg in bowl. Stir in greens. Pour into crust. Bake for roughly 45 minutes, or until lightly browned on top.

Weedy Foxtail Tabouli

1 cup foxtail seeds
1 cup purslane leaves (or parsley), chopped
(additional purslane leaves left whole for
garnish if desired)
½ cup wild onion (or scallions), chopped
2 Tbsp. fresh mint or spearmint

½ cup lemon juice
¼ cup olive oil
2 garlic cloves, pressed
¼ cup olives, sliced
lamb's quarter (or lettuce) leaves, whole

Separating foxtail seeds from stems and bristles:

Gather dry (brown) foxtail seed heads and place in a sturdy paper bag. Rub bag gently with rolling pin or hands until seeds feel loose. Pour seeds into bowl of water, skim off bristles, and remove or hand-separate any remaining stems or stalks.

Simmer prepared foxtail seeds in an equal volume of water for 12 – 15 minutes. Allow to cool. Place all ingredients except lamb's quarter/lettuce leaves and olives in a mixing bowl and toss together lightly. Chill for an hour or more before serving.

Wash and dry lamb's quarter/lettuce leaves and use them to line a salad bowl. Add tabouli and garnish with olives and whole purslane leaves.

Serves 4

Foxtail seeds are mature in early fall, when the seed heads and leaves turn brown. However, it can be harvested at any time after that, as seeds will remain fresh on the plant throughout much of the winter.

RECIPES

Tanyel's Yogurt & Purslane Salad

1 cup plain yogurt
2 or 3 cups of washed and roughly chopped
   purslane
2 cloves of garlic (mashed)
salt

Mix together and add a drizzle of oil before serving.

If desired, you can add chopped fresh dill or mint.

Serves 2–3

Recipe from Tanyel Turkaslan-Bulbul

Purslane & Potato Salad

1 lb. red or Yukon potatoes, either peeled or
   unpeeled and sliced into chunks
4 Tbsp. extra virgin olive oil
3 Tbsp. capers
6 cloves garlic, chopped
1 tsp. Dijon mustard
½ lb. purslane leaves, chopped coarsely
2 Tbsp. red wine vinegar
salt and pepper

Cover potatoes with water by at least an inch and season with salt and pepper. Bring to a boil and then simmer for about 20 minutes.

Sauté garlic in a large pan in olive oil and add purslane. Cook until tender, about 5 minutes.

In a medium bowl, add potatoes, garlic and parslane together. Fold in mustard, capers and vinegar and gently toss together.

Serves 4

Recipe from Kerri LaCharite

Purslane is at its most abundant in August and early September. Though it can be found and eaten as early as June, it might be hard to find enough leaves to make the full dishes.

89

RECICES

Strawberry Japanese Knotweed Pie

¼ tsp. salt
½ cup sugar
4 cups fresh or frozen strawberries
½ tsp. cinnamon
2 cups fresh knotweed, trimmed
of leaves and cut into ¼" lengths

1 tsp. cocoa powder
¼ cup all-purpose flour
1 Tbsp. lemon juice
4 tsp. cornstarch
pie crust

Preheat oven to 350°F (177°C).

Mix all ingredients in a large bowl. Turn into prepared crust. Top with layer of crust and bake for 35 – 40 minutes or until juices are thick and bubbly and crust is golden.

Recipe from Kerri LaCharite

Harvest Japanese knotweed in late spring when shoots are young and tender. Shoots can be 18" – 24" with a diameter of ¾".

❀

For a Little Girls' Play Date

Dolls' Salad
(semi-edible, non-toxic)

Gather wild strawberries. Place in small bowl with violets, wood sorrel, mint, dandelion leaves and flowers. Serve with Canadian hemlock cones as a main course.

SOURCE DIRECTORY

A good general resource site: www.gardenrant.com

I. Seed

- Bailey Seed Co. 800-407-7713
  www.baileyseed.com/clover.asp (for clover)
  Hobbs & Hopkins, Ltd. 503-239-7518
  www.protimelawnseed.com/products/fleur-de-lawn
  (for Fleur de lawn mix)
- Peaceful Valley Farm Supply 888-784-1722
  www.groworganic.com
- Ernst Conservation Seeds 800-873-3321
  www.ernstseed.com
- Outsidepride.com 800-670-4192
  www.outsidepride.com
- Gardener's Supply Co. 888-833-1412
  www.gardeners.com

II. Corn gluten (for organic weed control)

- Gardens Alive! 513-354-1482
  www.gardensalive.com; for Q&A about corn
  gluten, go to: www.gardensalive.com/article.
  asp?ai=753&bhcd2=1285954135
- Bradford Organics 800-551-9564
  www.bradfieldorganics.com/corngluten900.html
- Planet Natural 800-289-6656
  www.planetnatural.com/site/corn-gluten-meal.html
- Clean Air Gardening 888-439-9101
  www.cleanairgardening.com/organicfeed.html

III. Tools

Broadfork – good for aeration

- Johnny's Selected Seeds 877-564-6697
  www.johnnyseeds.com/
  p-5484-johnnys-520-broadfork.aspx
  (This is also a good seed company)

Reel mowers

- Fiskars 866-348-5661
  www2.fiskars.com/Products/Yard-and-Garden/
  Reel-Mowers/Momentum-Reel-Mower
  (They also make great clippers and cutting tools)

Composting supplies

- Gaiam 877-989-6321
  www.gaiam.com/category/eco-home-outdoor/
  outdoor/composting.do

Digging tools

- Cobrahead (weeder and cultivator)
  866-962-6272
  www.cobraheadllc.com
- Easy Digging 573-256-1858
  www.easydigging.com

These companies have not paid to be on this list.

91

INDEX

ACKNOWLEDGMENTS

FROM NANCY

I'm grateful to Paul Kelly and Catherine Dees for imagining this book into existence, and to Sheila Rodgers for the best kind of working partnership. Stomach and heart-felt thanks to Kerri LaCharite for her work on recipe development. Love and thanks to Brian, Emily, and Hazel, for patience and faith.

FROM SHEILA

My love and appreciation to my immediate family – Mark, Kirsten, Maisie, Liam, Megan, Joey and Molly, and also to my larger extended family. My sincere thanks to Nancy Gift for sharing her time, weed knowledge and sense of humor with me.

ABOUT THE AUTHOR

Nancy Gift serves as Acting Director of the Rachel Carson Institute at Chatham University, and is assistant professor of environmental science. Her winding academic career took her through biology at Harvard and weed science at the University of Kentucky and Cornell. This is her second book, her first being *A Weed By Any Other Name*. She lives with her family, 4 chickens, 1 cat, and a lawn full of many beloved weeds.

Nancy can be found online at **goodweedbadweed.weebly.com** and on her blog at **weedsandkids.blogspot.com**.

ABOUT THE PHOTOGRAPHER

Sheila Rodgers is a Visual Arts graduate from Chatham University and a Pittsburgh-based photographer. Her personal gardening motto is "Grass is overrated."

More of Sheila's photographs can be found at **srodgersimages.weebly.com**